MW01515419

A
SPARROW
CAME DOWN
RESPLENDENT

A SPARROW CAME DOWN RESPLENDENT

STUART ROSS

POEMS

A Buckrider Book

Buckrider Books is an imprint of Wolsak and Wynn Publishers.

Cover image: *The Mighty Sparrow* by Roy Green
Cover and interior design: Natalie Olsen, Kisscut Design
Author photograph: Delphine Roussel for Jennifer Rowsom Photography
Typeset in Tundra
Printed by Coach House Printing Company, Toronto, Canada

 Canada Council   Conseil des Arts
for the Arts   du Canada

 Canadian   Patrimoine
Heritage   canadien

 ONTARIO ARTS COUNCIL
CONSEIL DES ARTS DE L'ONTARIO
an Ontario government agency
un organisme du gouvernement de l'Ontario

The publisher gratefully acknowledges the support of the Canada Council for the Arts, the Ontario Arts Council and the Canada Book Fund.

Buckrider Books
280 James Street North
Hamilton, ON
Canada L8R 2L3

Library and Archives Canada Cataloguing in Publication

Ross, Stuart, author
A sparrow came down resplendent / Stuart Ross.

Poems.
ISBN 978-1-928088-11-0 (paperback)

I. Title.

PS8585.O841S63 2016   C811'.54   C2016-900676-X

This book is for Laurie,
my love

Ducking up and down she cast her quick bird's eye over the bushes at the audience. The audience was on the move.

VIRGINIA WOOLF
Between the Acts

These are my words.
They existed before I was born
but not in this order.

DAVID W. MCFADDEN
"My Words/Hamilton"

CONTENTS

POMPANO

And my mother is on the balcony
and my father is making cheese sandwiches
and my mother is writing a letter
that my father will discover
two months later in their bedroom
in Toronto, the morning
we're to bury her

she writes that
she is on the balcony
and he is making cheese sandwiches
and she says she feels treasured
and if ever there are grandkids
tell them she'd've loved them

and in five years my brother
dies in my sobbing father's arms
and my father one year after
and I cannot find the letter
my mother wrote in Pompano
but I remember the word *treasured*
it's how she felt, she said

    and palm trees sway in the hot breeze
    and butterflies called daggerwings drift past
    and sand skinks swim through millions of grains of sand
    and I – I am a pompano
    I am this forked-tailed fish
    I am this fish and I search
    for that letter in my mother's hand
    beyond the Atlantic coast

DOXOLOGY

A sparrow came down resplendent
from a bunch of clouds a string
trailing from its beak and
a fireman below watched this
though he couldn't see the string
from where he was the sparrow
came right toward him
where he stood in front of
the fire station the fireman
stood his ground as the sparrow
opened his beak and a piece
of string just a tiny piece of
white string came drifting down
the fireman opened his mouth
and the string sailed in it went
down his throat and into his
gullet as the sparrow winged
back into the sky resplendent
in the days that followed the
fireman didn't notice anything
much different except that now
he was a fireman with a piece
of string inside him and the
sparrow had said unto him
he remembered the sparrow
saying *they abide and they*
endure carry a piece of their
nest within you don't fuck
things up like you usually
do like how you wrecked
your family and the fireman
held out his palm and the sun
shone upon it and many
baby birds did there appear.

AUGUST 2008

for Laurie

I arrived with a jar of pickles.
The town was small.
We sat on your porch.

We saw a man pursuing the horizon.
The water in our glasses was crystal.
You read me a poem by Stephen Crane.

I read you a poem by Stephen Crane
and I said: "Is it good, friend?"
Now this is the strange part:

You leaned toward me
and the sky turned red. What then?

COLLECTED POEMS

for Richard Huttel

I am lying in bed, my dog
curled behind my legs, and
I'm reading *Collected Poems*
by Ron Padgett when I hear
her call from the bathtub,
"Hello, fried eggs!" It is no
particular occasion, not a
holiday or anniversary, but
I sneak out of bed and go into
the kitchen, pull a pan out
of the cupboard, put it on
the stove, drop in some butter,
etc., etc., until soon two perfectly
fried eggs await her on a plate,
flanked by salt and pepper
shakers, on our tiny kitchen
table. Soon the front door
slams and she is gone, and
not long after, the eggs are
cold. I have a great deal of work
to complete today, before
the weekend kicks in,
but I spend most of the day
replaying what happened
in the morning. The shout from
the bathtub, the eggs on the stove,
the front door slamming and
her little black car disappearing
around the corner. It is Friday.
Hello.

Young Adul is sitting in the field
reading a book. The book is about
a young boy who sits in a field
and reads a book. The sun is hot.
From somewhere in the village
trickles the faint sound of music.
Adul's father plays a horn. Suddenly
the book goes dark. At first Adul
thinks he forgot to charge it
and it has run out of electricity.
Then he remembers the village
has no electricity and his books
are made of paper. Therefore
it is just that he has been oblit-
erated by a bomb that missed
the village. He knows the village
has survived because he still
hears the music. Adul flaps
his arms and rises into the air.
He passes some neighbouring
countries, then finds himself
over the ocean. Soon he is landing
in the United States of America.
There are big moving pictures
stuck on the sides of buildings
that are taller than the tallest
tree that Adul has ever seen. The
streets are filled with cars and
trucks. There are neither
animals nor plants. Children
travel by jetpacks and their
books run on batteries. Soon
Adul arrives at an armament

factory. He is so small
the man at the door doesn't see
him brush by his knees. Inside
a man is at a desk. Adul peers
up at him and says, "Can you
unmake the bomb you dropped
on me so I can finish reading
my book? Also, I have to clean
out the hens' cage or my mother
will be unhappy." To the man
behind the desk, Adul's language
sounds like a crazy chimpan-
zee. In a country to the north
that Adul has never heard of
his language would sound like
a chimpanzed. I have placed
a cheap joke in a poem about
the death and misery caused
by Western imperialism. To
compensate, I will make Adul
alive again, sitting in his field,
reading his book to its very
end before he tends to
the hen droppings. He has
never flown. He has never
seen a building higher than
two storeys. In the distance,
he hears the music of his
father's horn. I open a beer.
Suddenly my beer goes dark.

MY MOTHER HAD A STORE IN OUR BASEMENT

My mother had a store in our basement.
Our basement had black and white tiles.
I threw a fork at my brother Owen
who stood at the top of the stairs.
I missed but splintered the door a bit
and all the Jewish women in Bathurst
Manor came down to my mother's store
and bought vases, dry flowers and frames.

In a room beyond the store was my father's
workshop: nails, a vise, hacksaws, levels and wrenches,
rolls of brown paper and hunks of Styrofoam.
And it smelled down there, of grease and spiders,
of heat from the cobweb-draped furnace. The furnace
had a small window at one end. I stared into the flames.
I took my friends down through my mother's store
and together we stared into the flames.

Up three floors, I shared a bedroom with Owen.
I lay in bed and thought of the furnace below.
While I lay there sleeping, a fire was roaring
in the room beside my mother's store.
The lawn was covered in snow.
Ice hung from the telephone wires.
My grandfather's teeth
sat on the edge of his sink,
dictating poems
to the night.

It was 1972. Weather was flying
around outside. Ken and I were thirteen.
We had both had our bar mitzvahs. Now
we were men. There was a chessboard
between us. Fred Reinfeld was our
favourite writer. Paul Morphy
blew our minds. We played chess for
thirty more years but we didn't get
any better. We were in Ken's house
on Evanston. His mother gave us
hot dogs and niblets. I subscribed to
Chess Canada but never read an issue.
Except that issue that said on the cover:
"Boris Spassky: These Are My Secrets."
Ken and his brother Lorne built a secret
maze out of cardboard boxes in their
basement. Ken's father had a book
on his shelf called *The Theory of Elastic
Stability*. In the article, Boris Spassky
said he could not share how he
demolished his opponents: "These are my
secrets." *The Theory of Elastic Stability*
is by Stephen P. Timoshenko. *Logical Chess:
Move by Move* is by Irving Chernev.
Many famous chess players have been
Jewish. Ken and I are Jewish. "Who
was Ruy Lopez?" I asked Ken. "A Spanish
priest, Ruy López de Segura was the author of
Libro del Ajedrez, published in 1561,"
Ken replied. As far as sports went,
Ken and I sure liked playing chess.
The chessboard has sixty-four squares.
Walt Disney died at sixty-five
in 1966. Contrary to popular belief,
they froze him not.

POEM BEGINNING WITH A LINE BY NELSON BALL

Hundreds of small black birds
clustered around a dictionary.
They sniffed the binding,
trailed their beaks along the crisp pages.
A man approached and the birds
took wing, sailing up into
the clouds. The man reached down
and clutched the dictionary.
He lifted it to his eyes, opened
it to a random page. The letters
on the page were birdseed.

QUESTIONNAIRE #1

Have you ever made a mistake?
I sent them to war with the best intentions.

Why didn't you think of the poor?
I wanted to preserve their dignity.

Do you hunt for food or for sport?
I am committed to interrupting the frightening diminishment of
the Arctic ice sheet.

Where did you hide the money you accumulated?
I trust the people, and the people's love for me.

Do you believe the ends justify the means?
I only pretended to make them think they were drowning.

Has the world's opinion of your country diminished?
They only pretended they thought they were drowning.

SONNET FOR DAVID

When I was sixteen I found *A Knight in Dried Plums*
by David McFadden, or maybe it was *On the Road Again*.
I had never seen poems like this, and the book smelled good.
I was in a library in North York playing hooky with Mark Laba
from our alternative school. The teachers didn't mind.
The poems made me gasp and taught me more than classes.
This guy's poems were crazy and they sounded like people talking!
Shove over, Rudyard Kipling and E. E. Cummings!

Now forty years have passed and I have lost my parents,
plus a brother and many friends, and caused a lot of hurt and
now I'm friends with Dave McFadden. I'm reading a stack of sonnets
he wrote through his aphasia, and I find myself gasping
and calling to Laurie, "You gotta hear this one! Just one more!"
And Dave's head floats through our front door and grins.

Big Monkey watches over me
as the blistering clouds bang
against my window and I dream
of you again and you are alive.
We are in a snow fort on my lawn
on Pannahill Road and we pretend
we are soaring through space.
The rumble of a 1967 Valiant
station wagon passing by
my driveway is the roar
of a meteor hurtling toward
earth and narrowly missing our
craft. We know now that
everyone will die except us,
because we are in space. Except
our ship has turned into a womb,
its hot, sticky walls pressing
against us until we can barely
move our arms. We are crushed
together like conjoined twins,
and because you are dead, I
wonder if I too am now dead
and I call out to Big Monkey
but he is bent over my desk,
rolling a sheet of yellow paper
through the platen of my
1952 Underwood, so intent
he cannot see us in the TV set,
our palms against the screen
from inside, and vertical hold
starts slipping.

IN IN MY DREAM

In my dream,
I see my brothers
turn a corner
across the road.
One is a dead brother.
I wake up sobbing
and tell you about it.
Then I wake up shaken
and tell you my dream
about waking up sobbing
after dreaming
that Barry and Owen
had turned a corner.

I STEP INTO THE CROWD

I step into the crowd. I am both more distinct from and more like everyone else.

I step into the crowd. Shoulders rub against my shoulders.

I step into the crowd. My talents are put to use by people with talents I don't have.

I step into the crowd. Our words disappear, but our voices become one big voice.

I step into the crowd. We form committees, but some of the committees never meet because there is a flamenco competition, or possibly a flamingo competition, my hearing's not so good.

I step into the crowd. We all look up suddenly into the roaring clouds.

I step into the crowd. I am astonished to discover we are all reading the same novel, *The Goalie's Anxiety at the Penalty Kick*, by Peter Handke.

I step into the crowd. I put my hands over my pockets to deter thieves.

I step into the crowd. We are all thinking something different.

I step into the crowd. We are kettled.

I step into the crowd. We stretch and yawn, then set off in different directions.

I step into the crowd. I pull dollar bills from my pocket and hand them out to children with birthdays – a dollar for every child.

I step into the crowd. Someone is watching us through a telescope, from that planet right over there.

I step into the crowd, and the crowd steps out of me.

POEM BEGINNING WITH A LINE BY JOEL LEWIS

i

In fact when this interview is concluded, I shall
take off my pants. I shall
shove my pants into the toilet down the hall. I shall
walk into the street in my underwear. I shall
wait for my bus. The way the trees
lean over the streets, it's like they're
conspiring. The telephone wires
vibrate. If you hire me, I won't
disappoint you. I will be an asset
to the organization. What is it again
that you do? The children in the playground
are armed. You can't get onto
the monkey bars. The garbage trucks
are eating everything in sight. My family
is starving. Thank you for considering
my application.

ii

I won't wait for my bus. The garbage trucks, it's like they're monkey
bars. The way the trees are eating everything is starving. Thank
you to the organization for considering the telephone wires. Walk
into the street, take off my pants. What is it again you can't get
onto? The children in the playground vibrate. In fact, when this
interview disappoints you I shall lean over the streets, conspiring.
My application is concluded, I shall if you hire me in my underwear.
I shall – I will be an asset, shove my pants into the toilet. I shall be
armed in sight. My family down the hall that you do. I shall.

MONKEY BARS 1966

i

The monkey bars command the playground a block from where
I live. I hang from them, the cold metal comforting against my
fingers and palms. My skinny arms stretch and stretch, and before
my feet touch the ground, I swing my legs so my feet sail over the
trees, over the tops of houses, chimneys of brick, TV antennas,
farther and farther, and far below, on a curb, a boll weevil draws
in its legs and dies. This is the world. It extends as far as the eye
can see. My friends walk along the sidewalk. The concrete is
hot against their bare feet. They stop and pull gum off the road
and eat it. They have big brothers, and their big brothers smoke
cigarettes. My feet reach their limit, and snap back across the sky,
right back to me dangling from the monkey bars.

ii

The girls hang out at the plaza. They stand in front of the pet shop and point at the lizards and rabbits in the window. Flakes of snow sail down from the sky. Just a few. This is the world. The boys stand at a safe distance and look at the girls. They all love the little one named Debby, even me. She lives in a big house on the edge of a ravine. I bicycle past her house sometimes, but if she's on her porch, I speed away. A boy named Larry has a mother with one arm. She only had one arm when she got married.

iii

The wooden bench at the bus stop is scarred with cigarette burns. Somebody's big brother did it. A bus pulls up and a man steps off. He wears a hat and carries a briefcase. Every day he steps off the bus, except on weekends. We don't know where he goes or where he's coming from. On weekends, we gather in front of the TV and watch cartoons and wrestling. This is the world. In the winter the monkey bars are covered by snow and ice. You can't climb on them. You'd be crazy to try. If you touch them, your hands get stuck. Even the firemen can't save you.

iv

When my brother sleeps, in the bed beside mine, he floats out
the window and through the streets. I try and try, but I can't do
it. He tells me the next day he floated past a window where a
girl inside was wearing a brassiere. He just flips his feet like he's
swimming and he can glide while he sleeps. I jump off my bed and
try to stay in the air, but I fall onto the floor. Our father appears
in our doorway. He says we'll be late for school. This is the world.
In school we sit in rows. Our houses sit in rows. Our streets are
all in rows. The stores at the plaza all stand in a row. At night,
there are station wagons in our driveways. But during the day,
our driveways are empty. Women criss-cross the road constantly,
visiting each other.

v

At recess all of the students pour into the schoolyard. I am among those who try to be invisible. There are boys in the schoolyard who roll their hands into fists. There are boys who knock you over while other boys laugh. There are boys who turn their eyelids inside out and chase you around the schoolyard. There are boys who hold your arms behind your back while another boy punches you in the stomach and calls you a homo. This is the world. One girl's father owns a slaughterhouse. She brings a jar containing a cow's heart to class one day, and another day a jar containing a cow's eyeball.

My grandfather says he is going "downtown." I picture a town you can get to only by riding down a very long escalator. He puts on a tie and a vest. He smells like he's shaved even though he still has bristles on his chin. I ask my mother if we will ever see Grandpa again. I follow him down the street. He walks toward the bus stop. Leaves are falling on us from the trees. The bus pulls up, and the door swings open. I watch my grandfather climb in. The trees are reflected in the windows of the bus, and the telephone wires, and the monkey bars, and the clouds that roar across the sky. Soon my grandfather disappears.

The mother and father are in the ground. The ground
is cold, even now, in March. They are Shirley and Syd,
my mother and father. There's something on the hard ground
above them. It's feet again. "It's feet," says Shirley. And
then they hear a voice. "It's him again, Shirl," says Syd.
Him is the voice that comes from up above where their
feet once were. It speaks haltingly in Hebrew, always
the same words, *Yisgadal v'yiskadash,* the words are
somehow familiar, as is the voice, but Shirley and Syd
don't understand Hebrew, never have, and soon
the voice, as always, becomes quiet, plaintive: "I
am doing…visited Norma…called a sparrow…
and Barry tries…miss the days…I hope you're…"
The voice cuts in and out. The feet are shuffling
back and forth. Soon the weight of small stones
on a much larger stone. And a few rows over
and a little bit west, Owen is in the ground.
Soon: the feet. The cracking voice. "…nine years
older…you would never…Barry's finally…"
and *Yisgadal v'yiskadash,* the words remind him
that, right, that's why he's in this cold ground, he
always forgets. He hears the click of a small stone
hitting a larger stone, feet fading, the grind of
a tractor in the distance, the barely perceptible
swish of a plane gliding through clouds
far above. He remembers telling his brother
Stuart, when they shared a bedroom on
Pannahill, that when he slept he could fly, he'd
just kick his feet and he'd glide above the trees.

POEM FOR TUESDAY (January 1, 2013)

It is 2013. We are returning to old values.

It is 2013. Cats are taped carefully to their dogs.

It is 2013. Clothes are self-cleaning, like dishes and ears.

It is 2013. There is a white man in the Black House.

It is 2013. Commander Snout has arrived to offer us the option of a second nose on our face or in a convenient nose purse.

It is 2013. The clouds are shaped like apologetic codfish.

It is 2013. When I try to shave, the mirror plays games with my face.

It is 2013. This has never happened before.

It is 2013. The prime minister is a sociopath flapping his arms in a vat of blood pudding.

It is 2013. Facts have been replaced by fast food.

It is 2013. A woman awakes to find her son climbing a birch tree outside the living room window, then getting unsteadily to his feet on a precarious branch and holding up a sign that says: "I want to be an appliance like my father before me."

It is 2013. You hang like a brilliant moon over a field of grateful cartographers.

It is 2013. The weather has made poetry unnecessary.

AL AT MOORES

Al at Moores menswear store in Ajax,
Ontario, is a pretty good guy. Not just
because he found me a nice Italian suit
for $199 ($270 with tax and alterations)
but because he found one *below* my budget
instead of trying to upsell me
like the guy in the Cobourg mall.
At first Al said "a little spare change"
would get me the really good suits
but I said I didn't have any
and he believed me.
Also, Al looks good in a black suit
and not like an undertaker.
He delivered his corny suit-seller's jokes
knowing they were corny. And he also
marked my sleeve cuff with a sliver
of white chalk just like my grandfather
Sam Blatt used to do, a tape measure
draped over his shoulders like a tallit.
When my grandfather was in Branson
Hospital dying, he scrawled
some Hebrew letters on a piece of
paper towel because he couldn't talk.
I still have the paper towel but I'm
scared to find out what the Hebrew
letters spell. The cheap suits all looked
cheap but Al kept trying, even after
the store had closed. It's the first
suit I've bought since 1972, the year
of my bar mitzvah. I told this to Al.
It was a bit of a test to see if he flinched
finding out I am Jewish. He didn't.

This suit is for my wedding. I won't
need a suit for my funeral. Al
will wrap me up in a plain
white shroud – *Tachrichim* –
and he'll suppress the impulse
to find me a matching tie.

POEM BEGINNING WITH A LINE BY MATTHEA HARVEY

There were girls waiting at the gate.
There were dogs waiting with the girls.
The gate waited in front of the cemetery.
The dead waited in their graves.

Have you written the girls a letter?
Have you read the books they're reading?
Did you read books when you were a girl?
Why do girls like to read?

I know a dog who reads about dogs.
I know a dog who loves a girl.
Most dogs read to the girls they love.
Most of the dead walk dogs past gates.

A girl climbs up on another girl's shoulders.
Another girl scales the girls, then another.
A girl can see beyond the gate.
The dead are asleep on the horizon.

EVERYTHING

You listen to terrible
poetry. I listen to
terrible poetry. Rod Steiger
listens to terrible poetry.
A squashed caterpillar
listens to terrible poetry.
The town crier listens
to terrible poetry. Emma
Goldman listens to terrible
poetry. The flaming sky
listens to terrible poetry.
I wrote a poem. I was
lonely. I wrote a poem
describing how I was
lonely. Many a person
said I should write a book.
The next day I wrote
one. I called it *Eschew
My Feet*. It was copyrighted.
It made my muscles
sore to write it. I went
to sleep. I dreamed
about everything.
When I opened my eyes,
everyone became
very emotional
all at once.

MAH-JONG

When I woke, I was an ant – no, an anvil – no, a plaster replica
of my own head. No, that was when I was sleeping. I wrapped
my arms around a tiny orchestra and squeezed music out of it.
My mother came down from heaven, where she'd been playing
mah-jong with the girls, and sang to me: *If you don't push
back your cuticles, cuticles, you will surely die.* She made me
mittens and a scarf, then returned to the game. I could smell
her perfume in the wool, and when I woke, I heard the clack of
mah-jong tiles in the living room, and I shuffled in wearing my
green pyjamas and stole some wine gums from the candy dish.
When I fell back asleep, I realized it had all been real. The sugar
echoed in my teeth.

I have walked a mile south and I have bought a kosher egg roll
at a store called Regina's and I bought it from Regina and I
have walked a few doors west. This is Wilmington and Sheppard,
where I once got called a "dirty Jew." I enter another store and it is not
Pinky's Chinese Food and it is not Paradise Pizza. I am eating my egg roll.
Plus did I mention I bought a potato latke, I am eating that too.
I am in De Havilland Bookstore and the smell of mouldy books
fills my nostrils and I smell Charlie Brown books and Hardy
Boys books and I smell a book from the TV show *Rat Patrol* and
I smell a book by Ogden Nash, it smells like poetry. The prices
are scribbled across the covers in black grease pencil: 45 cents,
75 cents, 15 cents, and the books are stacked all around me, every-
where I look there are paperbacks. I buy a *MAD* book and
Rat Patrol and the old man takes my dollar and his wife comes
out from the back room and gives me a tired smile and asks if
I found some good ones today.
                I hand her the books and she nods
at the covers and puts the books in a paper bag and my fingers are
greasy from the latke and I step out onto the sidewalk. South
of Sheppard are the Christians, and back north are the Jews and
I walk north until I get to Searle and I go knock on Murray
Nightingale's door. Everyone who lives in Murray's house
has red hair, but no one answers the door, and on Brighton
is Eric Cohen, and on Acton is Mark Wolfstadt, and on Combe
is Randy Sinukoff, and Sheldon Teicher is somewhere, and
Hedy Cohen, and Debby Burke, and Allan Wolf too, but I
head straight home, past the Beth Emeth Synagogue
where I will someday have my bar mitzvah, and
Rabbi Kelman has red hair too, and there is Wilmington Park
and there is Wilmington Public School and there is Bathurst
Manor Plaza, where my mother will kill a neo-Nazi in a novel
I write forty years later.
                And soon I am at 179 Pannahill,
up in my room, on my back on my bed, and I spill the books
out of the paper bag, right onto my chest, and the truth is

I will never read the *Rat Patrol* book, but I read the *MAD*,
and next week I'll go back for the Ogden Nash. The smell
of fried macaroni and cheese wafts up from the kitchen.
I won't eat it unless it's fried. My grandfather is two floors
down at his Singer sewing machine; his foot pumps
the cast-iron treadle. His veins are made of thread.

THE HANGING

My grandfather yells his Polish English
as my pyjama top swings
from the banister above
and his sewing machine
is silent in his dark room
and my mother puts her hand
on the back of my head,
tells me, "He saw the pyjama
and thought it was you,
that you had hanged yourself,"
and I went to my room,
gazed out at the snow
blanketing the Nefskys' roof
and pictured myself hanging
from the banister,
my pyjama sleeve tight
around my throat,
my grandfather pushing my feet aside
as he lumbers up the stairs
to eat his lumpy porridge.

FROM

From the briefcase, I withdrew two identical file folders.

From each folder, I withdrew a photograph of a woman.

From my mouth, I extracted a piece of gum and pushed it into a scrap of paper, crushing it into a ball.

From the time I was six or seven, I had chewed gum compulsively.

From the sky, which we could not see, thirty sparrows swooped low, almost skimming the roof of the building that housed my office.

From their beaks came the words of birds, and the occasional flash of bird-tongue.

From the clouds above the birds came a sprinkling of rain.

From out, seemingly, of nowhere, I said, "It's the same woman – both of them are the same woman."

From somewhere in the canyon of the other man's throat came the rumble of phlegm.

From the flapping of the birds' wings came a force that caused leaves to flutter.

From the depths of my memory came the image of a woman screaming, her fingers stuck in the door of the car.

From her womb had issued a son, and two years after I last saw him, he drove his car into a wall.

OH CY TWOMBLY WE LOVE YOU GET UP

I was thinking about the Chicago
White Sox and Stéphane Mallarmé
and I bummed a cigarette off Ben Shahn
while I wandered the Black Mountains
it was a Gauloise or maybe a Popeye
I didn't have a lighter either way and
it was getting dark and there was
some fucking thing in my shoe
a burr I think I stopped to get it out
leaning against a newspaper
box that all the Ghanaian poets were
leaning against and I stopped at
my favourite coffee joint and
bought a Pepsi and a coffee black
no sugar and drank one then the
other then the other then the other
and it started snowing and when
that happens I want to catch the flakes
and put them in a scrapbook and
take shelter under my neighbour's
porch with Debby Burke my Grade 2
crush but then I saw a huge
canvas in the intersection of
Bloor and Yonge and all
the hot dog vendors were gone
and there were no cars it was
four in the morning and a baseball
mitt lay in the centre of the canvas
Cy Twombly has collapsed and his
father Cy Twombly has collapsed
oh Cy Twomblys we love you get up

THE MILE-LONG FINGERS OF PREACHER JACK

Preacher Jack Lincoln Coughlin of Malden, Massachusetts,
levitates from the motel bed. He is Linda Blair in *The Exorcist*.

My head spins. Then he's Boris Karloff on his knees,
by the edge of a pond. "He plucked all the petals from the flower,

Stuart, and threw them in the water, and when he ran out of petals,
he threw in the little girl. *He* didn't know!" It is Toronto, 1979.

His band is clustered around the TV set, watching Dini Petty
host *Sweet City Woman*. "And then the villagers

came after the monster, waving their torches,
and he held the *poor* girl's *body* and *wept*." My tape

recorder captures Jack's two-hour monologue. Then I take him
to a couple of used bookstores on Queen Street East. He is

looking for books on Washington and Lincoln. He finds a keeper
and I snap a photo of him holding it to his chest.

That night, at Larry's Hideaway, lanky, tall and blond,
coated with a film of holy sweat, Jack preaches from the piano,

his mile-long fingers bashing out a barroom boogie-woogie,
his voice careening through the low-ceilinged, smoke-filled room.

And then: a brief lecture on Mahalia Jackson before
"Just a Closer Walk with Thee." Great God!

what a scene has just taken place! I am yet dizzy
with the remembrance of it. How slowly the time passes here,

encompassed as I am by frost and snow!

FACTS

A sunny early evening in Toronto. I'm driving
right by Dave and Merlin's place on College
Street when the door swings open and they
both step out. I wave through my open window
and their faces brighten when they see me.
But I have veered into oncoming traffic and
a streetcar nearly hits my Honda Civic. Cars
honk, I swerve. I think of how stupid Dave
and Merlin must think I am, back there
on the sidewalk. Then I'm awake. Of
course, it was a dream! Dave and Merlin
don't live on College, my Honda was
stolen years ago, and I'm already dead.

QUESTIONNAIRE #2

Which type of cloud do you like best?
I prefer the cloud shaped
like a childhood crammed
with *Archie* comics.

Did you enjoy reading as a child?
My father hid the flashlight
batteries at bedtime.

How many hours of sleep do you need to feel refreshed?
Every minute of sleep
is a minute wasted.

Where did you get that nice sweater?
I had hoped you'd ask
about Mother.

Where did you get the nice sweater?
I paid two dollars for it
at the Baby Manatees First
Thrift Shop. My mother's
name was Shirley.

How do you select produce?
That which has the deepest colour,
and whose flesh gives slightly
to the pressure of the thumbs.
This is something
my mother taught me.

Why did you never marry?
Yes.

LESSONS FROM 2014

For your information, when
you eat things they go into you.
I learned this last year.
This year, however,
I cannot write a poem. I just
can't do it. My dog skids
around on the ice outside,
I'm bleeding the radiator
with fifty leeches, seismologists
curl at the foot of my bed,
episodes of *F Troop* are shot
in my living room, guppies
do tricks in the depths
of my teacup, plus:

confusion is the basic unit
of all living organisms. It has
been dubbed the building block
of life. A single confusion
divides to produce two daughter
confusions. Let's pack a lunch,
pile into the station wagon
and sit in the driveway.

In closing, then:
Blank sheets of paper
scribble poems on me.
A lamp throws a shadow
into the wastebasket.
The radiance of the night
is just about endless.

1 January 2014

THREE IN A ROOM

A hospital room.
Yellow walls, three brothers.
Mother in bed.
Her wiry hands.
Him, him, and I.
Our terror.
The blasting of TVs.
On Mother's lips now, a smile.
Him fidgets, needs a smoke.
Tubes run from her arms, her thighs.
Machines beep and flicker.
Mother's watering eyes.
Dark rings vanish.
Lips dry, teeth dull.
Lips open.
"All three of you here," she says.
"In one room," she says.
Her hair is thin.
Has she ever been so pleased?
Him scrapes his chair.
We say nothing.
Father paces the corridors.

FIFTY-ONE

When I blink
everything loses a split second.
When I shut my eyes tight
the world hurtles into chaos
until I open them again
and there is order.
When I stick out my tongue
the volume of my tongue is displaced
elsewhere: for example, a farmer
in Botswana sees the tip of his
elbow or one of his baby goats'
hooves disappear. When I write
two lines of poetry, two lines
by Mark Strand become erased.
When I eat a spoonful of cornflakes,
something the size of a spoonful
of cornflakes comes into existence
somewhere else: maybe in the next
room, maybe in a small knitting village
in Portugal. When I think of something,
which happens only rarely, someone
from my Grade 5 class, maybe Sheldon
Teicher or Cecile Kafka, who I haven't seen
in forty years, forgets what he or she
was thinking. It drives them crazy.
They're in the middle of a conversation
and suddenly they stop mid-sentence.
"What were we talking about?" they say.
When I'm full of ideas, I cause an
Alzheimer's epidemic. On a train journey
to Breslau in August 1912, Alois Alzheimer
became suddenly ill. He died three years later
and was buried in the plot alongside
his wife, Cecilie. He was fifty-one.

STUART ROSS

after Lisa Jarnot

When you do grow up
you will know the names of your ancestors.
Lentils will sing you songs of praise
from the steaming bowl before you.
You will sleep eight full hours a night
and your teeth will brush themselves
and floss, your nostril hairs
will clip themselves. You will
be king of the monkey bars!
Your poems will be read
by apes. Clouds will assume
your shape so the rain will fall
only on you. A monster will reach
a claw from under your bed
and no one will hear from you
ever again.

They paid me $150,000 an episode to write a drama series about a hammer, a tadpole and a Q-tip.

This changed my life.

People rushed me on the streets, I lived in an airplane, I wore shirts made of celery and silk.

It's not like the work was easy.

The producers interfered with my scripts: "Make it more tawdry," they said. "Give the hammer a busty girlfriend."

I clung to my principles and held these guys off as long as I could.

This was my art, after all.

But they destroy everything, these people, they put rock salt in your porridge, they defrost your cat, they crawl all over your ham-laced running shoes.

In exile, I wore lavender robes and wrote autobiographies of Kim Novak.

Here it was winter year-round and we huddled by our woodstoves, playing card games and telling jokes.

Television had not yet arrived, and no one knew that I had been the most celebrated scriptwriter of the post–*My Mother the Car* era.

Oftentimes, while my family slept, I snowshoed to the edge of town, to the snow-swept fields of abandoned bathtubs, where I chose a tub and therein crouched, singing fragments of my bar mitzvah *parsha*, whose words sailed into the cold wind like chimney swifts startled by a clumsy bear.

Then I would pull myself to my feet,
and clap my wings against my body,
and the thunder was heard
across the nation.

POEM

It was night and we all
took poison pills.
The world was going to end.
It hit me: if I could just
stay awake, I'd live and see
the whole apocalypse.
I did.

In the streets,
rough boys threw
furniture at me.

A PRETTY GOOD YEAR

The gulls are barking
– Cobourg Harbour, 2 a.m.
The lighthouse blinks red.

*

Your voice on the phone
groggy with beautiful sleep
– hello, morning sun.

*

Under star-specked black
I thrust fingers into lake
– touch it to our lips.

*

Here is this moment.
There it goes. Now: another.
Your eyes are constant.

*

You ask for your iPod.
I offer to sing for you instead.
"I'll wear my iPod and
you sing," you say.

*

Out of hospital
into cool night: 4 a.m.
On my lips, your kiss.

*

Lucas Point

Waves crash on the shore
– I gather them in my arms,
bring them home to you.

*

Reading Robin Wood
to Laurie at 5 a.m.
Rain hits our window.

*

I lie awake while
wet tires roll over wet roads.
Faint light on your face.

*

I'm thankful but I'm
greedy and want to be thank-
ful for even more.

*

Laurie does yoga
two hours before surgery.
Sunlight on her head.

*

Passing Colborne

The 401: night.
Ahead, somewhere: ambulance.
Giant apple smiles.

*

O.R., 3 a.m.
Tiny tools snake through your veins
– staunch blood tsunami.

*

In the chemo suite,
you struggle to stay awake.
Soon you'll ring the bell.

*

Laurie's hair has flown.
I glide my fingers gently
over this new head.

*

"Overall," you say,
"it was a pretty good year."
Dog gives you a look.

POEM BEGINNING WITH A LINE BY GILLIAN JEROME

You live in me. We're eating well.
You invite some friends. I take a nap.
You drink in me. You watch cartoons.
The sun is red. The sky is black.

You read in me. I'm glad you read.
I'm glad you like the food I like.
You pace at night. A bus grunts by.
The snow is grey. The trees are bare.

You dream in me. I see your dreams.
I feel it when you wake in me.
You count in me. You count the days.
A finch waits on your windowsill.

Issie Laba is lowered into his grave beside
Freda, who arrived six years earlier. Issie
was ninety-seven, and an hour before
had been eulogized by each of his three
living sons. (Michael died decades ago.)
The ground is hard with the end of winter, but
not so hard that you can't dislodge a shovelful
of dirt and drop it into the grave. Mark stands
a metre away. Stuart puts his hand on Mark's
shoulder, something he's never done.
They've known each other for fifty-one
years but they're just kids. It doesn't
seem so long ago they played Green Ghost in the
Labas' bathroom, lights out, sliding the glowing
plastic ghosts on the game board till a space
turned out to be a hole and the ghost dropped down
like dirt on a grave. The rabbi's voice slides from
mourning to celebration, then back again, and then:
Yisgadal v'yiskadash... Meanwhile in the Sunnyside
section, Syd and Shirley sense something new
about the dirt: "The Labas are *both* here," says Shirley.
"I think it's coming from the Toronto Independent
Benevolent Association," says Syd. They
haven't been neighbours with the Labas for over
forty years. Funny what happens when you're dead.
Back at the burial, a guy with a steam shovel
finishes the job. Eddie, Marty and Mark are orphans.
They drive to Mississauga to sit shiva. Stuart goes
for a Chinese buffet, $7.49, on Wilson near Bathurst.

POETRY IS, DOT DOT DOT

Real poetry comes
from the heart, it
seeks to express a
truth, find beauty
in the ordinary. The
heart is an empty
Coke can dangling
from some fishing
line hooked onto
a flowerpot sitting
on the ledge of an
eleventh-storey
window. Truth is
a heap of losing
lottery tickets with
a lighter moving
toward it in slow
motion and that
was everything we
had, we have nothing
more. Beauty is the
hardest to describe.
It is three parallel
motion squiggles
coming from Dagwood
Bumstead's arm as he
demonstrates a judo
chop for Mr. Beasley
the postman and
Cookie, whose hair
has undergone
many changes over
the years. Remember
the strip where

Alexander runs
away to Syria to
join ISIS and
Dagwood builds
an eleven-storey
sandwich and he
and Blondie sit on
the sofa to watch
a Kurosawa film
on TV with Henry
Kissinger's dog
Spinee? A poet
is a special biped
who uses its art
to express its
deepest feelings
and also who has
a way of seeing
things other people
don't see and who
is wise and feels
things deeply plus
has a strong vocab-
ulary that its Grade
8 teacher Mrs. Pennell
was very impressed
by, also Mrs. Pass
from Grade 5,and
even Miss Acker
from kindergarten,
all women of keen
intelligence and
profound beauty
who enjoyed filling
out report cards.

QUESTIONNAIRE #3

What interests you most while you fly?
Movement amid the glistening dew below.

Do you feel remorse for the hurt you've caused?
My beak is handsome and I remain focused.

Where do the clouds go at night?
Is that a joke? My wingspan is greater than my life span. I tumbled
from the nest an orphan. One day the clouds will part and I will
careen up through them and into a cascade of flickering stars.

Did you write this book?
Are you finished with those worms?

I DECLINE, THANK YOU, PLEASE GIVE IT TO BERKSON, BILL

The pure pleasure of reading Bill Berkson's *Serenade* (Zoland Books, 2000; cover and interior drawings by Joe Brainard) while I'm lying in the claw-footed bathtub is such that I levitate. My body rises beyond the rim of the tub, then about another metre, till I can see sweet cobwebs flutter from the ceiling, and I hear the water drain below me, and drops sail down from my naked body, and as they fall they turn to various colours of paint and, landing in the tub, they make a portrait of Bill Berkson. His features are hewn and striking, and he wears a white hat, which the drops quickly change to brown with a white band. I raise a hand and brush away the cobwebs, "Fragile as the glitter on Dame Felicity's eyelid," and the ceiling opens, an Underwood typewriter lowering until it's hovering just over me, a sheet of white foolscap rippling on the platen. I type this poem, shave, dry myself off, pull on some jeans and a madras shirt, and win the Nobel Prize in Literature.

ONE FRIDAY IN INVERMERE

The enormous blue sky
tugs a red funnel of dust
from 7th Avenue and 12th.
One roadworker keeps drilling,
another bites into a sandwich.
Ham, probably. The clouds
have never tasted a ham
sandwich. The mountains
don't like ham. "Hey,
we're like inverted funnels
sucking the sky into the ground,"
one says to another. But
she doesn't say it in English.
This is only a translation.

WIGWAM

I am four foot three my arms
are crossed at my chest I am sitting
at a small desk and wearing an
Indian headdress made of construction
paper I have three feathers! I just got
my third feather for knowing how
to spell "chesterfield" my third feather
is yellow my other two are blue and
red these are what are called
"primary colours" – oh! I just got
another feather! I put one palm
forward and say "how" that's what
we Indians say "how" Miss Leibovic
is very pretty she has brown hair and
wears a brown dress or sometimes
a red dress and also stockings and
black go-go boots I want to kiss her
right on her pink lipstick lips she gives
us homework which is to list three Indian
tribes how they got their food and where
they lived and outside in the playground
I trip walking across the playground
and the ground is covered in gravel
and I get some gravel in my knee it goes
right under my skin and soon there is
infection and pus what a weird word
"pus" these were the days when *F Troop*
was on TV and *Gilligan's Island* when
you'd be watching TV in your wigwam
and the picture would start skipping
upward so you'd reach behind the TV
and twist a little knob called vertical
hold and on Saturday you'd crawl into

a big cardboard box and draw controls
and windows Stevie Rosen would
close the box flaps from the outside
and you would roar into space hurtle
into the future where you lived with
Miss Leibovic and she said to you,
"Time is too large, it can't be filled up.
Everything you plunge into it is stretched
and disintegrates." A wind hums
through the telephone wires.

AND OSCAR WILLIAMS WALKS IN

I'm sitting in my bedroom listening
to Linda Ronstadt's *Heart Like a Wheel*
and then Leo Sayer's *Just a Boy*
and after that Randy Newman's *Sail Away*
for which I read the lyrics on the record sleeve
while it plays, every word, even though
I've listened to it about a hundred times before
and my mother's in the kitchen burning steaks
and making mashed potatoes and she yells up,
"Stuart! Your friend is here!" and Oscar Williams
(as I later find out his name is) walks in
wearing a bow tie and John Lennon glasses and
says, "I see you like reading," and it's not because
I'm reading the lyrics to "Simon Smith
and the Amazing Dancing Bear" at that
moment but because – I follow his eyes –
one wall of my room is covered in bookshelves.
I find him pretty creepy even though
I have lots of friends who are older than me
mostly because of this poetry workshop
led by a guy named George Miller
I go to every Saturday with Mark Laba
where everyone is older than us.
"Have you ever read this?" asks Oscar
Williams and he holds out a mouldy copy of
Immortal Poems of the English Language.
"I saw you have a mother down there. My mother
was named Chana Rappoport and my father
was named Mouzya Kaplan. I am Williams
in the same way you are Ross. Have you ever
read this?" Oscar Williams asks and he holds
out a dog-eared copy of *The New Pocket
Anthology of American Verse from Colonial*

Days to the Present. "They're pretty good,
you know, they have poems by people like
Ezra Pound and Robert Frost and Edna St.
Vincent Millay and William Carlos Williams
and Oscar Williams of course. Do you want to go
hang out at the cigar store?" The album cover for
Sail Away has a big picture of Randy Newman's
face and I hold it up over my own face so it
looks like I am actually Randy Newman.
"Pardon me," says Oscar Williams, "I thought
you were Stuart Ross, teenage author of such
immortal poems as 'jesus tobacco' and 'Ritual
of the Concrete Penguins.' I died in 1964
so I sometimes get confused." And then he is gone.
Like it was a dream. I go downstairs where
my mother is opening a can of peas and say,
"Why did you let that guy in, Mom?" and she says,
"What guy? All that rock music you play is giving
me a headache and you hallucinations. Go wash
your hands, we're having dinner soon."
It is 1974. In forty-two years I will include this
poem in a book called *A Sparrow Came Down
Resplendent.* Barry and Owen sit down at the table,
and me and my mom and dad. We take turns
trying to pronounce "Worcestershire."

POEM BEGINNING WITH A LINE BY JAMES TATE

I was peeling an onion.
A man watched me through the window.
The window was built by my ex-wife.
An onion is round and tastes foul.
I forgot why I was peeling it.
I forgot what *peeling* meant.
I sat on the kitchen floor and cried.
The man's hand reached through the window
and clutched my heart.
My ex-wife burst through the door.
She shot the hand with a handgun.
I owed her my life.
"Let's try again," I said.
"It will never work," she replied.
She shook her head
and dead leaves drifted
from her hair.
I couldn't remember
where she kept her rake.

2,015 DISCRETE PORTIONS

I placed the potato on my plate
and cut it into 2,015 discrete
portions. This took me nearly
six hours. A neighbour peering
through my window yelled
something at me but I only
saw his mouth move. The potato
is not a metaphor. The number
2,015 was selected randomly.
Meanwhile – when you're my age,
meanwhiles are important
because they mean two things
can happen at once, crucial
when time is running out –
meanwhile, on my front lawn
something had appeared:
small and orange and batted
about by the unforgiving wind.
Above, the white blob of sky
convulsed and birds sailed out.
I sent a teetering robot to prod
at the orange thing, examine
it under a microscope, subject it
to various intelligence tests.
I thought at first it was
the fist of a plastic soldier
I'd played with as a child,
but it turned out to be
one two-thousand-and-
fifteenth of a potato. The potato
was sweet. The plate was made
of tin. The neighbour at my
window was made of cardboard.

I was made of regrets, sneezes and
diminishing possibilities. Laurie
will tell me this is depressing, I
shouldn't be so hard on myself.
Meanwhile, on the television,
which is made of a rectangle,
a black-and-white woman
handed a violin to a child in
a ghetto in Poland. The wind
subsided and snow began to
zigzag from the sky. Each flake
had several choices to make.

1 January 2015

HELLO, I'M A POEM ABOUT JOHNNY CASH

This is a poem about Johnny Cash
as the line above this one clearly states.
It stands in the centre of a derelict stage,
squints out at you, then grins.

Any poem about Johnny Cash
must refer to black, black shirts, black hats,
to Johnny's junkie days, and redemption
with June, to "I didn't do it, my truck did,

and it's dead, so you can't question it."
Must allude to Johnny meeting with Richard
Nixon, and to Carlene Carter and
Rosanne Cash, plus Carlene marrying

Nick Lowe, and to "The Beast in Me"
(a song Nick wrote for Johnny),
to God and prisons and dangling nooses,
and a train pulling out of a station,

and to Johnny's cover of "Hurt," and how
my dad saw himself in the mirror
the day before he died and he said,
"What's happened to me?"

He said, "What's happened to me?"
and sat back down on his bed.

AFTER PIERRE REVERDY

Look,
only one alarm clock is left.
It rings. There is no one to read
the time. Even the rodents
are dead. The wind searches
for a leaf to twang. All is dark.
The earth no longer bothers
turning. What difference
would it make anyway?
Lakes and ravines can't
tell themselves apart.
The books are full of words
but what's a word?
The night disappears
with a breath.

RESEARCH

This poem required no research.
When facts were called for, I invented them.
When was the dog painting made?
It was made in 1932. Who
made it? It was made by a monk
named Brother Owenjay.
Who was the first person to
walk on the moon? Florence
Nightingale, and second was
Winston Churchmountain. Poetry
is not hard. Anyone can write it.
"You're a poet, and you don't
know it." I never get tired of
people saying that. My dog
looked at the painting
of the dog I had just hung on the wall.
"I recognize the artist's work,"
she said. "That would have been
painted by Thomas Edison while
he sat in the electric chair, shortly
before his execution for the
murder of Man Ray." I asked
my dog what Edison's last meal
was. "A big juicy deer leg
torn from some roadkill
on Highway 6 just outside of
New Denver, British Columbia,"
she responded. I am on my
deathbed, and my dog sits
in a chair by my side. "Who
will give you treats?" I asked her.
"Who will walk you?" She held
my hand in her two front paws

and looked into my eyes. Her
own eyes were cloudy now.
She was an all-purpose dog.
"Worry not about me," she replied.
"I will find my way, and I will
never forget you." Just then,
the sun shouted through the window,
"I am gone!" and then it was dark.
I could see neither my dog
nor my dog painting, but I could
hear my dog breathe. Dogs breathe
through gills located just behind
their ears. Their ears were invented
in 1752 by Xenakis Metastasis.
The room is becoming cold. A June bug
is buzzing against the window.
My name was Stuart Ross.

ACKNOWLEDGEMENTS

I am grateful to my friend Buckrider editor Paul Vermeersch for pushing me toward the exact kind of book I wanted to do, and for many excellent suggestions: the lines of my poems are happy for his dedication to them. Thanks, too, to publisher Noelle Allen for her faith in this book, to copy editor Ashley Hisson and publicist Emily Dockrill Jones, and everyone else at Wolsak and Wynn, as well as Natalie Olsen of Kisscut Design for her sensitive treatment of Roy Green's (thank you, Roy!) fantastic painting.

Immense and endless gratitude to my wife, Laurie Siblock, for being such an honest and encouraging first reader of my poems, and for providing a model of profound love, creativity and thoughtfulness.

NOTES

As to the poems:

"Oh Cy Twombly We Love You Get Up" was written on Jake Mooney's dare.

"A Pretty Good Year" is for Laurie and the amazing family she brought me into.

Various endings (and more) salute Stephen Crane, David McFadden, Frank O'Hara, Jean-Paul Sartre and Mary Shelley.

Some of these poems have been published previously, and often in earlier forms. Thank you to the editors of the various print and online magazines, and the chapbooks and leaflets. Here goes:

"Doxology," "Three in a Room" and "Adul and the Magic Book" appeared on *The Lake*.

"August 2008," "Poem Beginning with a Line by Nelson Ball" and "One Friday in Invermere" appeared in *Stone the Crows!*

"Ruy Lopez," "Everything," "My Years in Exile," "Poetry Is, Dot Dot Dot" and "I Decline, Thank You, Please Give It to Berkson, Bill" appeared in *Fell Swoop*.

"Questionnaire #1" and "Questionnaire #2" appeared in *Unarmed*.

"Sonnet for David" appeared in *The Boneshaker Anthology* (Teksteditions, 2015).

"Make Big Monkey Writing Poems" and "Al at Moores" appeared on newpoetry.ca.

"I Step into the Crowd" appeared in *Wayward Arts*.

"In in My Dream" and "Poem Beginning with a Line by Joel Lewis" appeared in the chapbook *In In My Dream* (BookThug, 2014).

"Monkey Bars 1966" was commissioned by Catherine Cormier for the exhibition *Banlieue! Ordre et désordre* at Maison des arts de Laval, in August 2015.

"Poem Beginning with a Line by Matthea Harvey" appeared in *EVENT*.

"Mah-Jong" appeared in the chapbook *Nice Haircut, Fiddlehead* (Puddles of Sky Press, 2014).

"The Hanging" appeared in *The Malahat Review*.

"From" appeared in *jubilat*.

"Oh Cy Twombly We Love You Get Up" appeared on *Cosmonauts Avenue*.

"Fifty-One" appeared in *The Southern Testicle Review*.

"Stuart Ross" appeared as a leaflet from Puddles of Sky Press.

"A Pretty Good Year" appeared as a chapbook in 2014 from Nose in Book Publishing.

"Poem Beginning with a Line by Gillian Jerome" and "Poem Beginning with a Line by James Tate" appeared on *The Puritan*.

"Wigwam" appeared on *Synapse*.

"Hello, I'm a Poem about Johnny Cash" appeared in *Taddle Creek*.

STUART ROSS published his first literary pamphlet on the photo-copier in his dad's office one night in 1979. Through the 1980s, he stood on Toronto's Yonge Street wearing signs like "Writer Going to Hell," selling over seven thousand chapbooks. He is the author or co-author of twenty books of fiction, poetry and essays, as well as scores of chapbooks, leaflets and broadsides. Stuart was a member of the short-lived improvisational noise trio Donkey Lopez, whose CDs include *Juan Lonely Night* and the someday-to-be-released *Working Class Burro*. He is a founding member of the Meet the Presses collective and has his own imprint, a stuart ross book, at Mansfield Press. Stuart lives in Cobourg, Ontario, and blogs at bloggamooga.blogspot.ca.